T0208871

ARE YOU *Hungry* AND *Thirsty?*

Encouraging Women to Study God's Word

DONNIE WARFORD

WESTBOW
P R E S S®
A DIVISION OF THOMAS NELSON
& ZONDERVAN

Copyright © 2022 Donnie Warford.

All rights reserved. No part of this book may be used or reproduced by any means, graphic, electronic, or mechanical, including photocopying, recording, taping or by any information storage retrieval system without the written permission of the author except in the case of brief quotations embodied in critical articles and reviews.

This book is a work of non-fiction. Unless otherwise noted, the author and the publisher make no explicit guarantees as to the accuracy of the information contained in this book and in some cases, names of people and places have been altered to protect their privacy.

WestBow Press books may be ordered through booksellers or by contacting:

WestBow Press
A Division of Thomas Nelson & Zondervan
1663 Liberty Drive
Bloomington, IN 47403
www.westbowpress.com
844-714-3454

Because of the dynamic nature of the Internet, any web addresses or links contained in this book may have changed since publication and may no longer be valid. The views expressed in this work are solely those of the author and do not necessarily reflect the views of the publisher, and the publisher hereby disclaims any responsibility for them.

Any people depicted in stock imagery provided by Getty Images are models, and such images are being used for illustrative purposes only. Certain stock imagery © Getty Images.

ISBN: 978-1-6642-7215-6 (sc)
ISBN: 978-1-6642-7214-9 (e)

Library of Congress Control Number: 2022912665

Print information available on the last page.

WestBow Press rev. date: 07/29/2022

BSB:

The Holy Bible, Berean Study Bible, BSB Copyright ©2016, 2018 by Bible Hub Used by Permission. All Rights Reserved Worldwide.

CEV:

Scripture taken from the Contemporary English Version © 1991, 1992, 1995 by American Bible Society. Used by Permission.

ESV:

"Scripture quotations are from the ESV® Bible (The Holy Bible, English Standard Version®), copyright © 2001 by Crossway, a publishing ministry of Good News Publishers. Used by permission. All rights reserved."

NASB:

"Scripture quotations taken from the (NASB®) New American Standard Bible®, Copyright © 1960, 1971, 1977, 1995, 2020 by The Lockman Foundation. Used by permission. All rights reserved. www.lockman.org"

NIV:

Scripture quotations taken from The Holy Bible, New International Version® NIV® Copyright © 1973 1978 1984 2011 by Biblica, Inc. TM. Used by permission. All rights reserved worldwide.

NKJV:

Scripture taken from the New King James Version® Copyright © 1982 by Thomas Nelson. Used by permission. All rights reserved.

NLT:

Scripture quotations marked (NLT) are taken from the Holy Bible, New Living Translation, copyright ©1996, 2004, 2015 by Tyndale House Foundation. Used by permission of Tyndale House Publishers, a Division of Tyndale House Ministries, Carol Stream, Illinois 60188. All rights reserved.

KJV:

Scripture taken from the King James Version of the Bible.

ISV:

Scripture taken from the Holy Bible: International Standard Version®. Copyright © 1996-forever by The ISV Foundation. ALL RIGHTS RESERVED INTERNATIONALLY. Used by permission.

CONTENTS

PRAYER

Heavenly Father, my simple prayer right now is that you will use this book to speak to and bless the people who read this message. Send your Holy Spirit to convict each of us and motivate us to truly make you Lord of our lives. May we be forever changed with a lasting new determination to hunger and thirst for you constantly. In Jesus's name, I pray. Amen.

1

Bible Study Changed My Life

*I am a broken vessel allowing God to use me in whatever
way He sees fit for His honor, glory, and praise.*

Bible study has become an integral part of my daily
routine, helping me to grow and making a huge difference
in my life. This book was written to encourage *each* of
you and to show you ways that your relationship with
the Lord can deepen and thrive as you dig into His
Word.

Matthew 5:6 says, *"Blessed are those who hunger and thirst
for righteousness, for they shall be satisfied"* (ESV). And Psalm
42:1 says, *"As the deer longs [thirsts] for streams of water, so I
long for you, O God"* (NLT).

Deep down in your soul, do you *really* desire to
become a godlier woman and grow closer to God? Do
you truly desire "living water" to flow through you, or

do you hunger and thirst for righteousness? Most of us, if not all of us, would say of course without giving any thought to it.

I've been a church girl all my life. I read my daily devotional, prayed every day, followed several plans to read the Bible, and did multiple Bible studies. But I realized that I was mostly going through the motions with very little desire to hear what God was personally saying to me or learn how to apply His truths to my life. I could tell you what the Bible said on just about any subject pertaining to Christian living and principles. I even tried to keep in mind that *all* scriptures should have some application for godly living, because 2 Timothy 3:16 says,

> *All Scripture is inspired by God and is useful to teach us what is true and to make us realize what is wrong in our lives. It corrects us when we are wrong and teaches us to do what is right.* (NLT)

However, I mainly had the head knowledge, not the heart knowledge. In my daily personal time with the Lord, I would read a devotional and the scriptures prescribed in my Bible's reading plan, and then I would pray mostly empty prayers. I read my devotional each day out of convenience, so I wouldn't have to take the time to study the scriptures myself. My mind would often wander to other things. I really wasn't motivated, thirsty, or hungry for the Word of God like I knew a Christian should be. I found my Christian walk falling into the trap of routines and boredom.

To entertain myself, I started playing games on my iPad. After that, I searched for and entered several sweepstakes or giveaways. This opened my email address to numerous emails that required my time and attention, most of which contained articles that I *really* enjoyed reading. After handling all my messages, I opened Facebook. I scrolled through my newsfeed for a while, checking my notifications and looking through my messages. I was developing an addiction. I looked forward to hurrying through my time with God, so I could spend endless hours entertaining myself on my iPad. Then it was time to get up, fix lunch, and start my day. What a terrible waste of time! Can anyone else relate to this, or is it just me?

There are innumerable great Bible studies out there, but one day at my church, my small group leader and I discussed how the study we were doing was redundant. A lot of the scripture references did not apply directly to the topic we were studying. God inspired me to help my small group find a Bible study that would motivate me and the other ladies to dig deeper into God's Word. I began looking on the internet and Pinterest for Bible studies for women. Wow. "Ask, and ye shall receive" (John 16:24 KJV). I found all sorts of resources out there, even free ones.

While studying the material that I had discovered, I very quickly developed a desire to deepen my study of God's Word. I started writing down my experiences, along with suggestions on how to develop *heart* knowledge and how to apply God's principles to my life. He led me to numerous doctrinally sound resources.

A thirst and motivation started to grow within me, creating a desire to see what exciting nuggets of wisdom God had to show me in His Word. Jeremiah described this by saying the Word *"was in my heart like a burning fire"* (Jeremiah 20:9 NKJV). As a result of my searching and heightened awareness of God, He began speaking to me. I needed to share my experiences, thoughts, and scriptures with other women to encourage them in their daily walks with the Lord.

In order to be focused on God, know Him, and hear what He was saying to me, I needed to rid myself of needless distractions and get my priorities straight. That meant getting off Facebook, except to keep up with my family and groups that are pertinent to me; getting rid of my game apps; and unsubscribing from unnecessary emails. Also, I had to shut out all noise while I was spending my daily time with God, even Christian music, so I could fully focus on God's Word and allow the Holy Spirit to clearly speak to me. I had to silence my phone and put it out of sight, so I wasn't tempted to answer a call or return a text.

John Piper wrote an article called "How to Count It

All as Loss." One comment that really struck me was this: "Deal with everything in ways that draw us nearer to Christ." I needed to discover my "nearer to Christ" life.

Nothing is wrong with social media if we use it in moderation and don't let it distract us from doing what God calls us to do. But we must rid our lives of all things that unnecessarily prevent us from growing in faith, uplifting the Lord, or building our relationships with God. We are to be a people set apart from the world. In Philippians 3:7–10, Paul says the following:

> *But whatever were gains to me I now consider loss for the sake of Christ. What is more, I consider everything a loss because of the surpassing worth of knowing Christ Jesus my Lord, for whose sake I have lost all things. I consider them garbage, that I may gain Christ and be found in him, not having a righteousness of my own that comes from the law, but that which is through faith in Christ—the righteousness that comes from God on the basis of faith. I want to know Christ.* (NIV)

I am not suggesting you remove all the distractions that I had to. God convinced *me* to remove all things that prevented me from being in full obedience to Him. In doing so, I have discovered the "*peace … which surpasses all understanding*" (Philippians 4:7 NKJV). The Bible tells us that we can experience complete peace if we keep our eyes and hearts focused on God, not on earthly things.

What things do you need to lose or purge from your life in order to hunger and thirst for Christ and flourish in your relationship with Him?

Reflect and Respond: Make a list of things that you need to rid your life of that takes away precious quality time you can spend with God.

2

*Misplaced Desires, Priorities,
and Excuses*

Perhaps you don't even have a desire to seek God in your life. You selfishly ask yourself: What do *I* really want in life? Are you spending more time trying to maintain your outward appearance than trying to develop your inner character or grow your relationship with the Lord? First Samuel 16:7 says, *"For the Lord sees not as man sees: man looks on the outward appearance, but the Lord looks on the heart"* (ESV).

Perhaps you have too many things that require large amounts of your time for maintenance and upkeep. Do you seek material things, spend a lot of time shopping, or search for unnecessary things to fill a void in your life? In one of his daily devotionals, Dr. Charles Stanley wrote the following: "We all long for whatever we think will make everything just right. But that joy is 'synthetic' or 'artificial.'"

Think of a child's kitchen playset, the kind with plastic hamburgers, buns, and French fries. When little ones bring us a heaping plate of "food," we only pretend to eat. The same is true of our misplaced desires—they look enticing but will leave us empty.

The enjoyment of God is the only way our souls can be satisfied, and the voids can be filled. First Samuel 7:3–4 is Samuel's plea to the Israelites to get rid of their gods and to commit themselves fully to the Lord. Our gods could be our priorities in the wrong order, time-wasting activities, or the abundant stuff enslaving our lives and robbing us of valuable time. In Titus 2:12, God instructed *"us to deny ungodliness and worldly desires"* (NASB). Are you rejecting God by pushing Him aside and acknowledging someone or something else as your top priority? Matthew 6:19–21 says,

> *Do not store up for yourselves treasures on earth, where moth and rust destroy, and where thieves break in and steal. But store up for yourselves treasures in heaven … For where your treasure is, there your heart will be also.* (NASV)

To fully obey and please God, we must spend time in His Word and desire what He wants in our lives.

In one of Dr. Stanley's daily devotionals, he wrote:

"The sad truth is that many Christians would rather skip reading the Bible than skip something else in their daily routine. Yet, God's Word is the foundation of our faith, and we need to feast on it regularly if we're to thrive spiritually."

Satan's strategy is for you to be caught up in the details and pleasures of everyday life, distracting you so that you neglect your relationship with God. We make excuses, saying, "I don't have enough time for extra Bible study, because my life is already overloaded. I spend a few minutes each day reading a short devotional. After all, we're serving God. Isn't that what it's all about?"

We rationalize our excuses by thinking that we have jobs and families to take care of or are involved in ministries that take a lot of time. John Koessler stated that "being busy for God is not enough. Church activities can skew our view of God's personal plan and will for our lives."

As I was studying I Samuel 15, a sobering thought came to my mind about Saul's downfall as king of Israel and his failure to fully obey the Lord. Due to Saul's lack of *complete* obedience, the Lord called him rebellious and arrogant (1 Samuel 15:23 ISV). These are serious sins, because if we omit or fall short in Bible study, we are being rebellious and arrogant. We take the risk of suffering His consequences, like Saul. I read that "selective obedience [i.e., leaving off quality time alone with God each day] (emphasis mine) is just another form of disobedience." (author unknown)

I do not understand how God works in your life, but I know that He uses different methods to get our attention. What if He suddenly removed everything that is standing in the way of your spending one-on-one time with Him? We are on God's time. He gives us enough time in a day to accomplish everything *He* wants us to do. We owe Him quality alone time. He loves us and desires to spend time with us. He wants to show us His perfect will and plan for our lives. We need to apply the scripture that says, *"But seek first the kingdom of God and His righteousness, and all these things will be added to you."* (Matthew 6:33 ESV)

Reflect and Respond: Set a timer for ten to twenty minutes and begin your amazing transformation into the image of God. If you commit to at least ten minutes each day reading, meditating, and applying the Word to your life, you will develop a deep passion to find out what God has to say to you and what His will, purpose, and plan is for your life. You may discover that you want to carve out a longer time to spend with Him.

3

The Role of Forgiveness

When we study God's Word, we must have a clear heart and conscience to fully experience joy and peace. Failure to forgive others and ourselves hinders our spiritual growth and our intimacy with God.

Forgive others, including the unforgiveable.

Forgiveness is a choice we must make. God forgives us for the worst of our sins, even though we don't deserve it. Sometimes we must sincerely ask God to help us forgive. People hurt you or try to do you harm. A friend betrays you. Someone's negligence causes injury to or the death of a loved one. Maybe your spouse is unfaithful. God says, *"Forgive, and you will be forgiven"* (Luke 6:37 NIV). In Matthew 5:44, it says, *"But I say to you, 'Love your enemies and pray for those who persecute you'"* (ESV). When Joseph's brothers did all kinds of evil to him, he forgave them and eventually told them, "*You intended to harm me, but God intended it for good*" (Genesis 50:20 NIV).

Forgive God.

I have heard people say that they can't forgive God, because He took a child or loved one away with an untimely death, He *caused* them to lose their good-paying jobs because of COVID, or their toddler was diagnosed with an incurable disease. The ultimate selfless sacrifice God made for us was when he let his only son die on the cross out of love for every one of us. We must realize that God has the power to stop any adversity from entering our lives, just like he could have stopped Jesus's death.

But if God brings you to it, he'll bring you through it. God has *perfect plans* for our lives, many times including hardships, upheavals, and tragic events. His purposes are often beyond our understanding. We just need to *trust* Him!

What about your sins?

First John 1:10 says, "*If we claim we have not sinned, we make Him out to be a liar and His word is not in us*" (NIV). Are you doing things that make your weaker brother or sister stumble? Paul said, "*When you sin against them in this way and wound their weak conscience, you sin against Christ.*"

(1 Corinthians 8:12 NIV) Do you tell little white lies, gossip just a little, or spend God's money foolishly? Even though our salvation is unsevered, we still have human natures that allow Satan to influence and tempt us to sin.

I often pray that God will keep me from any willful sins that rule over me. I ask Him to convict me of any hidden or present sins. Frequently, I am convicted of some sin that I have harbored in my heart, such as impatience, pride, or jealousy. First John 1:9 says, *"If we confess our sins, He is faithful and just and will forgive us our sins and purify us from all unrighteousness"* (NIV).

Just asking the Lord to forgive our sins isn't going to be effective. We must be specific, admitting to God that our actions or thoughts are sins against Him. So confess your sins. Genuinely ask for forgiveness and repent.

An unforgiven sin is a barrier against growing close to God and being in full fellowship with Him. It puts distance between you and God. If a toddler sees his favorite snack laying on a table just out of his reach, there is a barrier of shortness. If the barrier of our sins is removed, we have full access to *"taste and see that the LORD is good"* (Psalm 34:8 NIV).

Reflect and Respond: First make a list of people you need to forgive, including God and yourself. It is often very hard to forgive, but God will help you and give you peace if you just ask. Then pray that God will reveal any of your hidden or present sins. As He exposes your sins, sincerely confess them to Him. Ask for forgiveness and turn from those sins.

4

Reasons for Bible Study

Dwight L. Moody once wrote, "The scriptures were not given to *increase our knowledge* but to *change our lives.*" (Emphasis mine)

Ephesians 6:17 refers to the Word of God as the *"sword of the Spirit"* (NIV). Allow the scriptures to *pierce* your heart and speak to you. Allow the Holy Spirit to perform His work in you, so you can do what He is calling you to do.

We all need to know how to live godly lives in an ungodly world.

Daily, we are in a spiritual warfare with Satan. He *"prowls around like a roaring lion looking for someone to devour"* (I Peter 5:8 NIV). We must know how to *"put on the whole armor of God, that [we] may be able to stand against the schemes of the devil"* (Ephesians 6:11 ESV). Only then will we be equipped with the Word of God as our weapon to fight back.

We need daily sustenance from God in order to thrive and experience abundant Christian life.

Just before my mother passed away, she refused to eat. She failed to absorb the vital nutrients necessary to maintain her life. When towns shut down, something similar happens. The sustenance of the once-thriving town has been cut off.

We need to *feed* on the Word, meaning we not only have to read the Scriptures but also absorb its nutrients and apply them to our lives.

If you are stranded in the desert or working outside on a hot day, you long for a cool drink to quench your thirst. Remember the story of the Samaritan woman at the well who Jesus requested a drink from. She didn't know about the thirst-quenching, living water that only Jesus could give. He said, *"If anyone thirsts, let him come to Me and drink. Whoever believes in Me, as the Scripture has said, 'Out of his heart will flow rivers of living water'"* (John 7:37–38 ESV). This living water is the Holy Spirit. If we allow Him to live within us, we will develop a spiritual hunger and thirst for the Lord. In addition, we will develop a strong desire to share what God has done and is doing in our lives. Abundant blessings flow to those who totally empower God to work in and through us.

We must hide God's Word in our hearts, so we learn how to be obedient to God and please him.

Reading scripture is not all that we need to do. (See Psalm 119:11). We must search scriptures like the psalmist who cried out to God: *"Open my eyes, that I may see wonderful things from Your law"* (Psalm 119:18 NIV).

In one of his daily devotionals, Dr. David Jeremiah said,

> "It takes a humble, worshipful, willing heart to discern the wondrous truths God has given in His written revelation. God has wondrous things to show us from His Word. But we must *humbly* yield our hearts to Him in order to truly see them and let them change our life." (Emphasis mine)

Allow the Holy Spirit to lead you in your search for nourishment and living water. Our time with the Lord—saturating ourselves in His Word, praying, and meditating—should be of the utmost importance to us, because it equips us with everything necessary to do His will. It determines His effectiveness and presence in our lives. By fueling our minds with truth every day, our hearts will grow to see God as a satisfying treasure that brings us numerous blessings.

The Word of God will also align our thoughts, choices, attitudes, and desires with God's will. If we don't faithfully seek out and follow God's plan for us, we become disobedient to Him. We veer off the righteous path and head toward a road of destruction.

We will find peace, happiness, and fulfillment that will forever change our lives.

With the help of the Holy Spirit, the Bible can teach us wonderful things. Several passages tell of the abundant and happy life we can have if we follow Christ's teachings. This doesn't mean we'll have a fountain of prosperity or a worry-free life. God's Word tells us that as long as we live in this broken world, life will have its trials and tribulations. But God will give us peace, comfort, and guidance if we seek to be obedient to Him.

Therefore, if you are sincerely thirsting and hungering to become the woman God intends you to be, this message is for you. Colossians 3:16 says, *"Let the Word of Christ dwell in you richly"* (ESV). Make a personal resolution to abide in Jesus daily by committing to habitual Bible study, prayer, and meditation.

Being intentional in your Bible study will allow the Word of God to infiltrate every part of your life, forever changing your life. Get excited about what God has to say to you, and desire to live according to *His* Word. Seek Him with all your heart. Do not stray from His commands.

Reflect and Respond: Write down three to four reasons why *you* need to study the Bible daily. Then post them somewhere you will frequently see them. Develop a consistent time to enjoy a precious "date" with the Lord each day.

5

Preparing for a Meaningful Bible Study

Effective, uninterrupted Bible study can be achieved if you first prepare your heart and spiritual space. Preparing our hearts is the most important step in truly spending meaningful time with the Lord. Prayer opens the door to the Holy presence of God.

Pray for God to reveal any hidden sins that need to be dealt with or that prevent you from hearing what He has to say to you.

Confess those sins, ask for forgiveness, and *repent*. Then ask Him for wisdom, discernment, and clarity. Ask Him to open your eyes and heart, so you can understand what you are studying. Finally, ask Him to fill you with the Holy Spirit, so you can hear what He is saying to you.

Gather the necessary tools for an effective Bible study.

These could include a Bible that you can mark up (i.e., *Life Application Bible*), a Bible commentary (such as *Matthew Henry's Commentary on the Bible*), a Bible dictionary, a concordance, different versions of the Bible, pens, pencils, and highlighters. In one of her blogs, Megan Allen pointed out a word of caution about Bible commentaries:

> "If we consult commentaries, devotionals, or others' thoughts too early, we don't allow the Holy Spirit the time to lead us into these new revelations. So, make sure you do your own diligent study first before consulting commentaries. Allow the Spirit to teach you first! Then, go for it! Compare your interpretation with some of the great Biblical scholars who have spent much time and effort sharing their wisdom with us."

Find a space where you can be alone with God.

Even if it is for just a few minutes, set up a place away from the hustle and bustle of the household. This is the time to put your phone on silent and out of sight. You may even have to get up earlier than everyone else to find that peaceful time that can only be had by being completely alone with God.

If we were truly honest with ourselves, most of us could admit that we are easily distracted. I have a problem with my mind wandering as I'm studying God's Word and praying. I often must ask God to help me stay focused and remove any distractions that interfere with my time with Him.

I love the old hymn "In the Garden." It's about coming to the garden *alone* in the early morning hours and being able to hear the sweet voice of God. Even the birds hush their singing. In that quiet alone time with Him, we can truly hear His voice. Things of the world fade as we turn our focus on Him. In her blog *Garments of Splendor,* Christin said, "The best part of waking up isn't to the aroma of freshly brewed coffee but rising to meet each day with God."

Reflect and Respond: Prepare a quiet, special place in your home where you can meet and be alone with God. Place your tools nearby. Make it an inviting space that you will look forward to each day.

6

Choosing Topics and Getting Started

Choose a topic, scripture, chapter, character, or book of the Bible, that God lays upon your heart and that interests you. Even the Old Testament is relevant in our lives, giving us stories about loyalty, opposition, and consequences. It also gives us examples of what pleases God. It reveals God's heart, which is gracious, kind, and loving. It teaches us He is a holy God. Romans 15:4 says,

> *For whatever was written in former days was written for our instruction, that through endurance and through the encouragement of the Scriptures we might have hope.* (ESV)

God is the same yesterday, today, and tomorrow. His Word is just as applicable to our lives today as it was when He inspired writers to pen the Holy Bible.

If you don't know where to start, pray that God will lead you to what He wants you to hear.

To find what God wants *me* to study, I keep an electronic folder handy to write down ideas. When I listen to a sermon; read a verse, chapter, devotional, or Christian article; or even attend a Bible study, something often sparks my interest. I also find many captivating topics on my favorite Christian websites. If I'm searching for a set of scriptures related to a topic and don't know where to find them, I go to the internet. I search this phrase: What does the Bible say about _____? I fill in the blank with the topic I am studying. To find references or scriptures I only remember bits and pieces of, I use an app called Bible Hub. At the top of the page, I enter what I can remember, like "equipping for every good work." I try to find all the resources I can, including sermon topics from some of my favorite preachers, Christian websites, or apps.

When I come across scriptures that are commands from God about Christian living or have special meaning to me, I like to write them down in my electronic folder. I review them periodically, so I can hide them in my heart and apply them to my life or use them to help others.

Always write down everything you are studying.

You may ask if it's necessary for you to write down what you are studying. I have found that if I don't write down my studies and review them often, it is like seeing my mascara smeared underneath my eyes, because I failed to remove it the night before. Eager to get my coffee made, the next morning, I distractedly walk away and forget that I am undeniably falling short of the glory of being an attractive-looking wife for my husband.

Also, if I don't have time to complete a study in one sitting, writing it down allows me to go back and review the previous day's work for continuity and context. And it makes it easier to pick up where I left off. In addition, it helps me reflect and meditate on God's Word as I apply it to my life.

Begin your study with an open and humble heart.

Be sensitive to what the Holy Spirit is trying to say to you. You'll engage in the most wonderful, life-changing journey you've ever experienced as you grow closer to God and find His perfect will, purpose, and plan for your life. Romans 12:2 says,

> *Do not conform to the pattern of this world, but be transformed by the renewing of your mind … to test and approve what God's will is - good, pleasing, and perfect will.* (NIV)

End your study with prayer and meditation.

Pray that God will help you apply what you have studied to your life so you will grow closer to Him each day. Pray that the Holy Spirit will help you meditate on God's Word throughout the day. Thank Him for opening your heart up to Him today.

Reflect and Respond: Using the guidelines above and the suggested Christian websites and apps in chapter 9, make a list of topics, scriptures, characters, and books of the Bible that you would like to study.

7

Sample Bible Study

Begin each Bible study with prayer, as described in chapter 5. Choose your topic or scriptures.

I chose Ephesians 4:32.

Read the passage slowly, underlining or highlighting key words or phrases.

(As demonstrated below, I like to number the keywords and phrases in the passage to coordinate their definitions, explanations, or applications for easy quick reference and correlation.)

"And be kind[1] and compassionate[2] to one another, forgiving[3] one another, just as God also forgave you in Christ[4]" (Ephesians 4:32 CSB).

Write down any background information or outside resources necessary for understanding the passage. Look up words in a Bible dictionary that you don't understand the meaning of. Write the word and meaning down.

I am commanded to be kind, compassionate, and forgiving. To be <u>kind</u>[1] means that with love in my heart, I must be courteous, nice, and humble toward everyone in an outward expression. To be <u>compassionate</u>[2] means that I am to suffer with another out of sorrow and love. Lastly, because God has forgiven me for my sins by sending His only son, Jesus Christ, to die on the cross as payment for my sins[4], I must obey God *and* <u>forgive others</u>.[3]

Write down things you need to change in your life. Don't forget to work on those changes.

I need to be <u>nicer</u>[1] to Jo, being patient with her, even though she uses me and just talks, talks, talks.

I need to have more <u>compassion</u>[2] for people when they fall on hard times, even if they may have created the bad situation themselves. (i.e., homeless people)

I need to <u>forgive</u>[3] Mary for all the hurt she has caused me by spreading a lie about me.

I need to thank God *daily* for saving my soul and sending His Son as a sacrifice and payment for my sins.[4]

Write down any applications for your life or what you need to share with others.

- Always be kind to *all* people, regardless of their race or socioeconomic status.
- Always be compassionate toward *all* people.
- Always forgive *all* people, regardless of how they have treated me.
- Do unto *all* people what I would have them do unto me.
- God is sovereign. He can give me peace, even amidst a storm.

Pray, thanking God for his written Word, wisdom, and the Holy Spirit to convict you. Praise Him for speaking to your heart. Ask Him to help you meditate on his Word and apply it to your life. Ask the Holy Spirit to help you carry through with what actions you must take to follow through with what God lays upon your heart.

8

Hunger and Thirst for God's Word

Are you satisfied with hearing God speak to you by only listening to a sermon on Sunday or reading a short devotional each day? Are you willing to miss all that God wants to reveal to you through His Word by being a mediocre Christian? Or will you join me in a fabulous journey of hungering and thirsting for more of Him?

Let us learn how to live an abundant and victorious life for God together, discovering the treasures and wisdom that He has stored up for us in His Word. The all-encompassing Bible is our *personal* life-guiding manual written by God.

REMEMBER: *If you're not growing in your walk with the Lord, you're stagnant, headed away from God's protection, or dead.*

Reflect and Respond: Pray that God will create a burning desire to *continually* hunger and thirst for more of him within your heart. Truly look forward to digging into his Word every day.

My Prayer

Heavenly Father, I thank you for your personal guidebook, which teaches us what is true and what is wrong in our lives. Your Word corrects us and teaches us to do what is right, while leading us toward a growing relationship with you. I thank you for sending your son to die on the cross—the ultimate sacrifice for our sins—so that we could be saved and become your children. Thank you for saving my soul. When you are finished with me on earth, I have an eternal home prepared for me in Heaven, so I can live with you forever. I thank you for your Holy Spirit that lives within me, convicts me, and enables me to live a righteous and faithful life. Also, I thank you for all who have read this booklet. I pray that this message will move in their lives and inspire, motivate, convict, and encourage them to continually grow closer to you. I pray they find your will, purpose, and plan for their lives. I hope this book creates a deep, burning desire that is never completely satisfied when they study your Holy Bible. Lord, I pray that you get the honor, glory, and praise for all you have done and are doing in my life. In Jesus's name, I pray. Amen

9

Additional Help

Always check your resources against the Bible to make sure they align. Along with the suggestions mentioned in this chapter, use the internet as discussed in chapter 6 or Pinterest to search for Christian Bible studies.

Christian Websites

arabahjoy.com

bible.knowingjesus.com

billygraham.org

bloggersforthekingdom.com

davidjeremiah.org

desiringgod.org

faithgateway.com

garmentsofsplendor.com

intouch.org

kayleneyoder.com

ladiesdrawingnigh.org
livingbydesign.org
meganallenministries.com
proverbs31.com
ptv.org
timewarpwife.com

BIBLE APPS

1. Knowing Jesus—this app has several versions of the Bible; concordances; topics; thematic Bible words, phrases, and names; parallel chapters; cross-references; and devotionals.
2. Bible Hub—this app has several versions of the Bible, a Bible library, cross-references, chapter outlines, commentaries, maps, and other Bible study tools.
3. Open Bible Info—this includes a topical Bible, Bible verse search, and Geocoding (maps of identifiable places mentioned in the Bible)
4. Desiring God—this app offers inspirational articles, messages, books, and podcasts
5. Right Now Media—this app requires a paid subscription, but it's often subscribed to by your local church. It contains many Bible studies and inspirational videos.
6. Billy Graham Evangelistic Association—this app includes Bible studies, devotionals, and Biblical guidance on many topics.

7. In Touch—this app has current and archived sermons, radio broadcasts of Dr. Charles Stanley, devotionals, and topical resources.
8. Turning Point – sermons, radio broadcasts, and devotionals of David Jeremiah.
9. Pathway to Victory—with this app, you can watch, listen to, and read TV sermons. It also has radio broadcasts and daily devotionals from Dr. Robert Jeffress.
10. Access More—this app offers faith-based podcasts and videos, as well as access to some Christian radio stations.
11. Bible Study Tools—this app has dictionaries, commentaries, encyclopedias, concordances, lexicons, Biblical topics, and more.

Suggested Folders

You can find books or articles that will give you information to fill up these folders, but I pray that they will originate from your searches through scriptures and your desire to grow in your walk with the Lord. You can choose which ones might be beneficial in your life. You'll probably think of other folders that you would like to use. These might be godly legacies that you leave to future generations.

1. *My Bible studies.* Refer to the chapter 5 of this book for some suggestions.
2. *Words to hide in my heart.* If an airplane pilot suddenly has something go wrong with the engine or navigation system, he often doesn't have time to consult the manual. He must recall his training to know what to do. Being equipped with God's Word in your heart provides you with your own manual to rely on. While studying the Bible, we need to write out scriptures to commit them to memory and hide them in our hearts.
3. *Topics to study.* Keep a continuous list as God speaks to your heart.

4. *Names of God.* This could also include names that refer to His nature.
5. *Promises of God.* By clinging to God's promises, our faith will grow, and we will be able to face each situation with perfect peace.
6. *Commandments.* This could also include rules for godly living.
7. *Prayer journal.* It's necessary for me to keep a prayer journal, so I can remember to pray for all the people and circumstances needed. A digital journal works best for me, because as circumstances change, I can update each entry. This prevents me from having two or more related entries in different places. Do what works best for you but remember that we should always start with praise and thanksgiving, followed by confession, asking for forgiveness, and repenting of our sins. Then we should pray for others and, lastly, for ourselves.
8. *Examples of God speaking to me.* This could be through His Word, a sermon, a devotional, a prayer, or when seeking godly counsel. But make sure that it's not just your desires or Satan speaking. It *must* align with the Bible.
9. *Sermon notes.* I usually listen to several sermons each week. When I write my notes down, I also include scriptures, topics for further study, and helpful information for my other folders.

All my suggested folders can be done digitally. You will have more flexibility in arranging the entries, but it is important that you constantly review them for motivation, remembrance, necessary corrections, and meditation. I prefer putting each of my folders in Microsoft Word documents and naming them. They are so much easier to locate and make any changes to.

ABOUT THE AUTHOR

Donnie Warford felt a calling to share what God is doing in her life. She has plans to start writing inspirational articles for social media. Her passion is to motivate women worldwide to develop a close relationship with God and be obedient to His plan for their lives. She has been actively involved in her local church most of her adult life. She taught middle school math in Central Arkansas for 17 years. Warford and her husband, Ray, are retired and enjoy spending time with their four children, twelve grandchildren, and two great-grandsons.

Printed in the United States
by Baker & Taylor Publisher Services